Compensation for Loss of Pension Rights

Employment Tribunals

Guidelines prepared by a committee
of Chairmen of Employment Tribunals,
the Government Actuary
and a member of his Department

Third edition

London: TSO

Published by TSO (The Stationery Office) and available from:

Online
www.tso.co.uk/bookshop

Mail, Telephone, Fax & E-mail
TSO
PO Box 29, Norwich, NR3 1GN
Telephone orders/General enquiries: 0870 600 5522
Fax orders: 0870 600 5533
E-mail: book.orders@tso.co.uk
Textphone 0870 240 3701

TSO Shops
123 Kingsway, London, WC2B 6PQ
020 7242 6393 Fax 020 7242 6394
68–69 Bull Street, Birmingham B4 6AD
0121 236 9696 Fax 0121 236 9699
9–21 Princess Street, Manchester M60 8AS
0161 834 7201 Fax 0161 833 0634
16 Arthur Street, Belfast BT1 4GD
028 9023 8451 Fax 028 9023 5401
18-19 High Street, Cardiff CF10 1PT
029 2039 5548 Fax 029 2038 4347
71 Lothian Road, Edinburgh EH3 9AZ
0870 606 5566 Fax 0870 606 5588

TSO Accredited Agents
(see Yellow Pages)

and through good booksellers

© Crown copyright 2003
ISBN 0 11 3226241

Second impression 2005

Printed in the United Kingdom for TSO
N17642C   C6   2/05

The committee

David Sneath
Regional Chairman , Employment Tribunals, Leeds

Colin Sara
Chairman, Employment Tribunals, Bristol

Chris Daykin
Government Actuary

Adrian Gallop
Actuary, Government Actuary's Department

Table of contents

1. Introduction

1.1 This is the Third Edition of this Booklet which was last edited in 1991. The original Booklet received judicial approval in **Benson –v– Dairy Crest Ltd (EAT/192/89)** but the Second Edition was criticised in **Clancy –v– Cannock Chase Technical College & Parkers [2001] IRLR 331** where Lindsay J. President of the Employment Appeals Tribunal said:-

> "The rest of Mr Clancy's appeal is dismissed for the reasons we have given but we would not wish to leave the case without adding a plea. It arises especially now that the cap is £50,000 and because full pension compensation is therefore more likely to require to be accurately computed than it was in the past. Our plea is that careful consideration needs to be given to whether the 1991 guidelines can still be relied on to give the valuable help they have done in the past or whether a fresh edition ought not to be prepared if the tribunals up and down the country are to be given the assistance they deserve in this "most difficult element" of the calculation of loss in unfair dismissal cases."

This criticism and the removal since 1991 of any statutory limits on compensation in discrimination cases led to the formation of the present working party.

1.2 In re-drafting the previous Edition we have tried to steer a middle course between over-simplification and over-elaboration. We have come to the conclusion that a distinction has to be drawn between the normal run of tribunal cases, where the amount of compensation is limited and the pension element is, therefore, comparatively small and those few cases, many of them discrimination cases, where the sums involved are considerable.

1.3 We have, therefore, developed alternative approaches. On the one hand we have retained the method set out in the previous editions, which has received considerable support from Chairmen and, indeed, from the bodies consulted about this Booklet. We call this *the simplified approach.* Meanwhile we have added a new approach, which we call *the substantial loss approach* which will be appropriate to those cases where the tribunal is considering "career loss" of a particular employment. This approach makes more use of actuarial tables than *the simplified approach.*

1.4 The structure of this booklet is that at Chapters 2 and 3 we make some general remarks about pensions provision. Then in Chapter 4 we set out the decisions which have to be made by tribunals in deciding which approach to take. Chapters 5 to 7 explain how assessment should be made under *the simplified approach* while Chapter 8 sets out how to make the assessment under *the substantial loss approach.*

2. State Pension Provision

2.1 The State Pension payable by the State may comprise the Basic State Pension, a Graduated Retirement Benefit and an Additional State Pension payable pursuant to the State Earnings-Related Pension Scheme (SERPS) and, from April 2002, the State Second Pension (S2P). State Pension benefits are normally payable from the State Pension age (currently 65 for males and 60 for females, although the female State Pension age will be 65 from 2020 and will be increased gradually from 60 to 65 between 2010 and 2020 for those born between 1950 and 1955 – see Appendix 3 Table 3.1).

2.2 **The Basic State Pension**

This pension is flat-rate and therefore independent of earnings levels. Provided that certain contribution requirements are met, the Basic State Pension is payable to everyone over State Pension age, with the amount depending on the number of contributions paid or credited.

2.3 **Graduated Retirement Benefit**

Graduated Retirement Benefit (GRB) is based on the amount of graduated National Insurance contributions paid by the employer and employee in the period between April 1961 and April 1975. The amount of an individual's GRB varies according to the number of units of graduated contributions paid by them. GRB payments are usually very modest and will soon cease to be of any significance for people in the active labour force.

2.4 **The State Earnings-Related Pension Scheme ("SERPS")**

This pension is earnings-related and varies according to an individual's earnings in respect of which he has paid full National Insurance contributions as an employee between April 1978 and March 2002. This is also called "Additional State Pension". It was based on earnings between the Lower Earnings Limit and the Upper Earnings Limit (£72 per week and £575 per week respectively in 2001–02, the last year in which SERPS benefits accrued).

2.5   **State Second Pension ("S2P")**

Following the enactment of the Child Support, Pensions and Social Security Act 2000, SERPS benefits ceased to accrue from April 2002 and were replaced from that date by the State Second Pension (S2P). Initially, the benefits accruing to employees earning less than £25,600 (in 2003–04, and increasing thereafter) will be higher under S2P than they would under SERPS. However, for those reaching State Pension age after a date yet to be specified, it is expected that the benefit payable will effectively become a flat-rate benefit.

2.6   **Minimum Income Guarantee and Pension Credits**

Currently, people aged 60 or over on low incomes and with savings of less than £12,000 have their income increased to the minimum income guarantee. From October 2003 the Minimum Income Guarantee will be replaced by the Pension Credit. This will guarantee the same minimum income of £102 per week for single pensioners and £156 per week for a couple (in 2003–04 terms). However, in addition, where pensioners have income from other sources, the 'clawback' will be at a rate of 40%, rather than the 100% used with the Minimum Income Guarantee. Thus, pensioners with modest savings will not lose one pound of benefit for every pound of pensions or other savings they have built up. From age 65 people with incomes up to around £139 a week (£204 for couples) will receive some benefit through the operation of Pension Credit. These limits will be increased annually.

Contracting Out

2.7   Since its introduction in 1978 it has been possible for employers to contract out of SERPS those employees who are members of a final salary occupational pension scheme which satisfies certain criteria. National Insurance contributions payable in respect of employees who are members of such a scheme which is contracted-out are paid at a lower rate than that payable for employees not in such a scheme (employers also pay National Insurance contributions at a reduced rate).

2.8   Before April 1997, a final salary scheme which was contracted-out had to provide a Guaranteed Minimum Pension ("GMP") as a substitute for the Additional State Pension. The GMP was broadly equivalent to the Additional State Pension paid under SERPS and was the minimum amount of occupational pension that must be paid from a contracted-out final salary scheme. Often such a scheme would provide benefits that were higher than and additional to the GMP. For service prior to 6 April 1997 it is possible for someone who had been contracted-out to build up rights to a partial Additional State Pension as well as their Basic State Pension and the pension from the contracted-out scheme.

2.9 GMPs no longer accrue for service after 6 April 1997. From that date, final salary schemes wishing to contract out have to pass a Reference Scheme Test (RST). This requires that the pensions provided by the scheme are broadly equivalent to, or better than, those required by the RST.

2.10 Employees who have served all their pensionable service as members of a contracted-out scheme will receive the Basic State Pension paid by the State as well as a pension from the contracted-out scheme. When the State Pension is paid, the Basic State Pension and Additional State Pension have an inflation protection element built into them. While an employee is still employed, any accrued GMP element increases broadly in line with wage inflation. For pension relating to the tax years 1988–89 and later, the GMP element of the retired employee's pension after retirement will be increased in line with price inflation, subject to an upper limit of 3% per annum. Where inflation exceeds that amount any excess will be paid by the State through increasing the Additional Pension.

2.11 From 6 April 1988 it has been possible for occupational money purchase schemes to be contracted-out of SERPS. Since July 1988 individual employees have been able to make their own arrangements to purchase an Appropriate Personal Pension and use this to opt out of SERPS and/or their employer's pension scheme. In this case both the employer and the employee pay the full rate National Insurance contributions and at the end of the tax year to which the contributions relate, the Inland Revenue pays an age-related rebate (which increases with age) direct to the pension scheme for investment on behalf of the employee. Since April 2001 employees have also been able to use a stakeholder pension to contract out of SERPS.

2.12 As with SERPS, it is possible to contract out of the new S2P either by means of an occupational or personal pension scheme or with a stakeholder pension.

Potential loss

2.13 Accrual of State Pension benefits may be interrupted if an employee is out of work, although credits are available for the Basic State Pension whilst in receipt of Jobseekers Allowance or Income Support and some credits are available for S2P. Assuming that an employee is re-employed without too long a delay, the loss of Basic State Pension arising from dismissal is likely to be nil or relatively small. Thus we recommend the assumption that there is no loss of Basic State Pension in respect of a dismissed employee. The onus will then be on him or her to show otherwise.

2.14 The Working Party have, however, identified a new area of potential loss which arises when an employee who is not in a contracted out occupational or personal pension scheme is dismissed. Where a dismissed employee is not in a pension scheme or is in a scheme which is not contracted out, he is liable to lose the Second State Pension element for the period that he is out of work. The full method of calculating this is set out in section 7.5 and Appendix 3.

3. Occupational Pension Schemes

3.1 Occupational pension schemes fall into two main categories: final salary (otherwise known as defined benefit) and money purchase (otherwise known as defined contribution). An increasing number of schemes are a mixture of the two but it will usually be possible to calculate the two elements separately.

Final salary schemes

3.2 These are schemes where the amount of pension paid is based not on the contributions made by the employer or the employee, but on a proportion of the earnings of the employee for each year of service (e.g. $10/60^{ths}$ of final salary after 10 years in the company pension scheme).

Example:

A joined the company scheme in 1980. He retires in 2000 and his salary in the year before his retirement is £30,000 p.a. The pension from the scheme is based on $1/60^{th}$ of his final year's salary for each year. Therefore his annual pension will be $20/60^{ths}$ of his final year's salary, i.e. £10,000 p.a.

3.3 In most cases the employee makes a contribution of a fixed percentage of his income into the fund throughout his employment. The employer usually agrees to make contributions to the fund at least matching those made by the employees but such as to ensure that the benefit costs are met. There is usually little difficulty in establishing the contributions currently made by the employer as a percentage of the total pay-roll but this may vary from year to year depending on how well the pension fund is keeping up with the demands that are likely to be made on it. Sometimes the employer may be enjoying a contribution "holiday", with reduced, or even zero, contributions for a period. Such a temporary reduction should not be taken into account for the purposes of compensating an employee for loss of pension rights. Where there is a lack of accurate evidence, or where the current contribution position is anomalous, the Government Actuary advises that on average the overall standard contribution for a good scheme is 20% of the pay-roll, made up, in a contributory scheme, as to 15% from the employer and 5% from the employee. It is important to note that the employer's contribution is not earmarked for the pension of any individual employee and the pension that an employee actually receives will not necessarily be proportional to his and the company's contributions.

3.4   On the face of it non-funded schemes (particularly publicly financed schemes like the Principal Civil Service Pension Scheme) might seem to be different from normal final salary schemes because, as there is no fund, there is no need for contributions to be paid in advance to meet the accruing benefits and benefits could just be paid as they arise. However, an appropriate level of employer contributions is usually fixed by the scheme's actuary as though they were funded and should be easily obtainable. These non-funded schemes, therefore, can be treated in the same way as any other final salary scheme. It should be noted, however, that they tend to be more generous in the way in which they increase as a deferred pension before retirement and as a pension in payment during retirement. Typically public service schemes increase by the full percentage increase in the cost of living index whereas private schemes are only obliged to increase up to 5%. In a period of low inflation this may be seen as a minor issue.

3.5   Not all final salary schemes use the same pension fraction. However, by far the most common fraction in the private sector is $1/60^{th}$ of final salary per year of service and most public sector schemes have a fraction of $1/80^{th}$ but also provide a tax-free lump sum benefit equivalent to three years' pension payments. Members of private sector schemes usually have the right to give up part of their pension in return for a tax-free lump sum of a similar amount to that provided by public sector schemes. Taking this into account, a private sector scheme with $1/60^{th}$ benefits can be roughly equivalent to a public sector scheme with $1/80^{th}$ benefits. Some schemes use the best of the employee's last few years for the calculation of final salary; others may use the average of the last few years or even a career average, which may be substantially less favourable to the employee. However, the essence of a final salary scheme is that the employee's pension is based on his earnings and length of service and not directly on what the employee or the employer have contributed to the fund.

3.6 "Additional Voluntary Contributions" (AVCs) have existed for many years and employers offering occupational final salary schemes must allow them to be made, if the employee wants to top up the company pension. AVCs usually operate on a money purchase basis, even where the main scheme is a final salary scheme. As such they should be treated in the same way as company money purchase schemes (see 3.9 below). However, some schemes (mainly public sector) allow employees to buy extra years. If this has been done the additional years already bought will be put into the equation of loss of final salary pension rights as if the employee had actually worked those extra years.

3.7 AVCs are usually made by the employee alone. They, therefore, have no significant bearing when future loss of pension rights comes to be considered, unless the employer was making some contribution towards their cost. They are not 'portable', however, and the loss of the facility to make AVCs could in some circumstances be regarded as a financial loss to the individual, where they were relying on being able to top up their pension in this way. Any loss is likely to be in the form of additional charges paid out to the pension provider in setting up a replacement scheme.

3.8 "Free-Standing Additional Voluntary Contributions" (FSAVCs), introduced in October 1987, are in effect separate and, therefore, 'portable' money purchase plans and should be dealt with as Appropriate Personal Pension plans. There will be no loss to be taken into account unless the employer was contributing towards the cost.

Money Purchase Schemes

3.9 **Company Money Purchase Schemes:**
These are quite different from final salary schemes. The pension payable is directly related to the contributions made by the employer and the employee to the fund over the years. In the past they gave inadequate compensation for the effect of inflation and became unpopular, but there is

a move back to them, because they enable the employer to know exactly how much the scheme will cost each year and to budget accordingly, whereas a final salary scheme may be an open-ended commitment.

Example:

A joined the company in 1982. He retires in 2002. Over the 20 years he and his employers have contributed £20,000 to the scheme, but let us say that the accumulated contributions are now worth £50,000. For this, on annuity rates current at the time of writing, a pension of about £3,600 per annum can be provided. The amount of the pension, of course, varies not only according to the success of the investment policy but also with the age and the sex of the annuitant, whether dependants' benefits are also purchased and the interest rates current at the date of retirement.

3.10 **Personal pension plans including individual life insurance backed schemes:**
The idea of these plans, very simply, is that the employee and the employer or either of them makes contributions to a private pension policy with an insurance company or other pensions provider of the employee's choice. On retirement the employee then receives an annuity based on the value of his personalised fund. The main difference between these plans and company money purchase schemes is that it is usually the employee and not the employer who decides where the money is to be invested. Whilst employers are required to contribute to occupational plans, this is not the case in respect of personal pensions. Appropriate Personal Pension plans can also be used to contract out of SERPS and S2P.

3.11 FSAVC's are a form of personalised plan designed as a private top up for employees in company pension schemes (see paragraph 3.8).

3.12 **Stakeholder pensions:**
Stakeholder pensions were introduced under the Welfare Reform and Pensions Act 1999 with the aim of encouraging private pension provision. Stakeholder pension schemes provide money purchase benefits only, but the employer is not required to contribute to the arrangement. All

employers must provide access to a stakeholder scheme for their employees unless there are fewer than 5 employees or the employer already offers a suitable pension scheme. Although this means that it is likely that an increasing proportion of employees will have access to a pension scheme of some sort, there may not be any increase in the number of cases of loss of pension rights on dismissal, since it is unlikely that all employers will contribute to stakeholder pension plans.

Life Assurance Cover

3.13 Many pension schemes provide, or have separate schemes associated with them to provide, life assurance benefits for their members. In appropriate cases it may be just and equitable or otherwise appropriate to compensate former employees for the loss of the benefit of belonging to such schemes by awarding as compensation the average market rate for providing equivalent cover.

4. Pension Loss – Introduction

4.1   Anyone who leaves pensionable employment before retirement is known as an "early leaver". Persons who are unfairly dismissed or are the victims of discrimination and lose their jobs are examples. The effect of leaving early will depend on whether the scheme is a final salary or a money purchase scheme.

4.2   With a money purchase scheme, whether company or personal, the fund built up to the date of leaving by the contributions of the employer and the employee remains invested for the employee's benefit. Accordingly, what the employee loses on dismissal is the prospective value of the further contributions that his employer would have made. As far as his own future contributions are concerned, there is no loss, since he can use the compensation awarded for lost earnings and/or any earnings in a new job to pay into a pension scheme associated with his new employment. If he is not re-employed, he should still be able to make contributions to a stakeholder pension or enjoy similar advantages from investing in an ISA.

4.3   A person dismissed who is a member of a money purchase scheme may be required to pay a penalty for leaving the scheme early. This is also a loss directly attributable to the dismissal, but it is easily quantifiable. Apart from this he does not lose any part of the current value of contributions already made by his employer and himself.

4.4   In a final salary scheme the position is much more complicated. On being dismissed the employee loses the prospective right to a pension based on his final salary. In most cases that come before the Tribunal, however, he will be entitled to a deferred pension. It is the difference between this deferred pension (including any cost of living increases and other benefits) and the pension and other benefits that he would have received had he not been unlawfully dismissed that constitutes his loss.

4.5   The applicant's loss of pension rights on dismissal is the difference between the pension he will receive in due course and the pension he would have received if he had not been dismissed. The value of the former can only be truly assessed when he dies and the value of the latter includes a number of imponderables. Although the benefit does not come into payment until the applicant retires, it is still a fringe benefit derived from the employment like a company car or private health insurance, albeit considerably more valuable once accrued.

4.6 Often the applicant has not found other employment by the date of the hearing. In this situation the tribunal is engaged in the highly speculative process of deciding when he is likely to find other employment and how much he is likely to earn if and when he does. Forecasting the likely pension, if any, in such employment is just one part of this highly speculative process, which includes deciding whether the applicant would have left his previous job anyway and whether he would have been promoted if he had not been dismissed.

4.7 The key choice to be made by the tribunal is whether to look at the whole career loss to retirement which can then be discounted to allow for the eventuality that the applicant would not have remained in the employment throughout, or to look only to the next few years and assume that by that time he will have obtained comparable employment either with a similar pension scheme or a higher salary to compensate. Tribunals have tended to find in many cases that the applicant would obtain comparable employment within a fairly short period, ranging from 3 months to 2 years. Where the likely period of unemployment was longer the tribunal would quickly find that compensation had reached the previous statutory limit of £12,000, so that assessing future loss over a period of years was largely an academic exercise. However, the increase in the limit in respect of compensatory award for unfair dismissal to £50,000 (now £53,500) and the removal of any limit in discrimination cases and some unfair dismissal cases require, where appropriate, an approach akin to that adopted in personal injury cases.

4.8 The Ogden Tables were prepared by the Government Actuary's Department for use in typical personal injury cases. They enable the courts to convert a total loss of employment continuing to retirement into a lump sum based on the annualised loss of earnings, age at trial and likely retirement age of the individual. They also include tables which assess loss where the loss of earnings is for a fixed number of years. Whilst these Tables are just a guide, they are used routinely by the courts unless there are circumstances calling for a different approach. These Tables have occasionally been used by tribunals to assess future loss of earnings whether whole or partial. The EAT in **Kingston upon Hull City Council –v– Dunnachie (No. 3) EAT/0848/02** have laid down guidelines for their use in that context, but have specifically excluded compensation for loss of pension rights. However, the guidelines in that case may be helpful in deciding which of the two approaches in 4.10 below to use.

4.9   In a case where the Ogden Tables are being used to assess future loss of earnings, there is a clear need for a comparable approach to pensions using similar assumptions. There may also be cases where the loss of earnings is slight and the loss of the pension is the most significant aspect of the compensation.

4.10   We consider that, in assessing future pension loss, the tribunal has to select one of two approaches, which we will call *the simplified approach* and *the substantial loss approach*. As we have indicated, the decision by the tribunal as to which approach to use will be a crucial one. It has led to considerable debate in the consultation process and the final conclusion will be a matter for the tribunal. It can, however, make a substantial difference to the amount of compensation under this heading.

4.11   *The simplified approach* is set out in Chapters 5, 6 and 7. It involves three stages – (a) in the case of a final salary scheme, the loss of the enhancement to the pension already accrued because of the increase of salary which would have occurred had the applicant not been dismissed, (b) in all cases, the loss of rights accruing up to the hearing and (c) the loss of future pension rights. These last two elements are calculated on the assumption that the contribution made by the employer to the fund during the period will equate to the value of the pension (attributable to the employer) that would have accrued. In the case of a final salary scheme, it may be necessary to make an adjustment to the employer's contribution as discussed in section 6.5. No such adjustment is necessary in the case of a money purchase scheme because the scheme is personal to the employee.

4.12 *The substantial loss approach*, by contrast, uses actuarial tables comparable to the Ogden Tables to assess the current capitalised value of the pension rights which would have accrued up to retirement. There may be cases where the tribunal decides that a person will return to a job at a comparable salary, but will never get a comparable pension see **Bentwood Bros. (Manchester) Ltd. –v– Shepherd [2003] IRLR364**. In such cases *the substantial loss approach* may be needed even where the future loss of earnings is for a short period. But it must be remembered that loss of pension rights is the loss of a fringe benefit and may be compensated by an increase in salary in new employment.

4.13 Experience suggests that *the simplified approach* will be appropriate in most cases. Tribunals have been reluctant to embark on assessment of whole career loss because of the uncertainties of employment in modern economic conditions. In general terms *the substantial loss approach* may be chosen in cases where the person dismissed has been in the respondent's employment for a considerable time, where the employment was of a stable nature and unlikely to be affected by the economic cycle and where the person dismissed has reached an age where he is less likely to be looking for new pastures. The decision will, however, always depend on the particular facts of the case.

4.14 More particularly, we suggest that *the substantial loss approach* is appropriate in the following circumstances:

(a) when the applicant has found permanent new employment by the time of the hearing and assuming no specific uncertainties about the continuation of the lost job such as a supervening redundancy a few months after dismissal; further, the tribunal has found that the applicant is not likely to move on to better paid employment in due course;

(b) when the applicant has not found permanent new employment and the tribunal is satisfied on the balance of probabilities that he or she will not find new employment before State Pension age (usually confined to cases of significant disability where the applicant will find considerable difficulty in the job market);

(c) when the applicant has not found new employment but the tribunal is satisfied that the applicant will find alternative employment (which it values, for example, with the help of employment consultants) and is required then to value all losses to retirement and beyond before reducing the total loss by the percentage chance that the applicant would not have continued to retirement in the lost career. See **Ministry of Defence –v– Cannock and Others [1994] ICR 918** et al. subject to our comment below.

The simplified approach becomes inappropriate in these cases because there is a quantifiable continuing loss which can be assessed using the pensions data and Tables 1 to 4 of Appendices 5 and 6. These tables use factors similar to those in the Ogden Tables for personal injury and fatal accident cases. Although tables for pension loss are included in those tables, the tables in this booklet use some different assumptions to those underlying the Ogden Tables (see Appendix 2).

5. *The simplified approach* (1) – loss of enhancement of pension rights accrued prior to dismissal in final salary schemes

5.1 When a person who is a member of a final salary scheme is dismissed or leaves for any other reason, he is entitled to a pension payable at what would have been his retirement date as an annuity for the rest of his life. This is referred to in this booklet as a "deferred pension".

5.2 In the most common form of private sector final salary scheme, an employee when he retires receives $1/60^{th}$ of his final salary for each year he has worked for the employer. For the employee retiring at the scheme's normal retirement age there is a maximum of $40/60^{ths}$. Frequently part of this pension is commuted to provide a lump sum.

5.3 The early leaver receives a deferred pension representing $1/60^{th}$ of his final salary (at the time he leaves) for each year he has worked for the employer (providing he has 2 years' service – if not, he usually receives repayment of his own contributions). The Pensions Schemes Act 1993 requires this deferred pension to be revalued in line with increases in the cost of living index up to the retirement age, when the pension comes into payment, subject to a cap of 5% a year over the accumulation period. (There are separate revaluation requirements for that portion of any deferred pension representing a guaranteed minimum pension.) Even with this revaluation, the deferred pension is likely to be much less than if it had been based on the final salary which the member could have expected to have had if he had remained with the company until retirement.

Example:

A worked for his employers for 15 years; he left, aged 50, on 1 December 1985 with a final salary of £10,000. His basic deferred pension was 15/60^{ths} of £10,000 = £2,500 p.a., payable from his retirement age 15 years later at the age of 65. By the time he reached retirement age, the cost of living index had increased by

56% (about 3% a year), so the pension which came into payment was £3,900 p.a.

Alternative example:

Instead of leaving he stayed with the company for another 15 years when he retired at 65 with a final salary of £21,000 (an increase of about 5% a year). His pension was £10,500 a year, of which £5,250 is referable to his first 15 years service.

5.4   By leaving early he has lost £1,350 a year from retirement to his death in respect of his first 15 years of service. This is the case whether or not he obtains fresh employment with identical salary and identical increases and with an identical pension scheme. There will be a corresponding reduction in any lump sum on retirement and any widow or widower's benefit.

5.5   What he has lost, however, is not necessarily the £1,350 a year pension difference between the two examples in 5.3. For example, he might well not have stayed with the company until retirement, even if he had not left at 50 years of age. He might have left or been sacked or the company might have gone into liquidation. On the other hand, he might have ended up as managing director with a salary of £100,000 a year and a pension of £50,000 a year. Alternatively he might have moved to a new job where his pension could be transferred in such a way as to preserve the full value of his past years of service. Who knows? Nevertheless his real loss on leaving could be substantial and there will usually be a loss arising from the difference between earnings revaluation of the accrued pension rights if he remained in service up to retirement age and the cost of living revaluation (capped at 5% a year) of the deferred pension.

5.6   Part IV of the Pension Schemes Act 1993 entitles a person to require his ex-employer to transfer the value of his accrued pension either to a similar scheme run by a new employer or personally to make other arrangements meeting the prescribed requirements (Para 13(2) of Schedule 1A to the Social Security Pensions Act 1975 as subsequently amended).

5.7   The transfer value is calculated in accordance with Regulations which refer in turn to the guidance note "Retirement Benefit Schemes – Transfer

Values (GN11)." This gives the actuary a certain amount of discretion which has been enlarged to the employee's disadvantage by recent amendments or, exceptionally, the pension fund trustees may, if they wish, be more generous to early leavers than the law requires. However, our understanding is that the transfer value is an actuarial figure which is intended to represent the present value of the deferred pension he can anticipate.

5.8   In theory, he should be no better or worse off by taking the transfer value and re-investing it than if he chooses to leave the deferred pension in the fund. However, it does create the additional possibility that the employee will find a better private pension fund to put his money into or that the transfer values will be assessed on a generous basis, or, on the other hand, that the new scheme may credit the transfer value on a less generous basis.

5.9   A common fallacy is the belief that an employee does not lose financially if his pension is transferred from his old employer's pension fund to his new employer's pension fund. In fact the transfer value will usually be assessed on the basis of the value of the deferred pension, as in the first example, and will not take account of the additional benefits that he might have received based on salary increases if he had stayed on to retirement age, or, usually, the value of any discretionary post-award pensions increases. Meanwhile, the scheme receiving the transfer value will allow for the fact that salary is likely to increase up to retirement age and may charge for the cost of discretionary post-award increases, so there may be no advantage to be gained from taking a transfer value. It follows that, where an applicant from the private sector has taken a transfer value to a new pension scheme, he will still need to be compensated for loss of enhancement of accrued pension rights as described in part (b) below. Transfer values operate more favourably than this between the public sector pension schemes.

(a) No compensation at all

5.10 We consider that in respect of certain categories of cases it would be just and equitable not to make any award of compensation in respect of loss of enhancement of accrued pension rights. In particular, we recommend there should be no compensation for loss of enhancement of pension rights in cases where the applicant is fairly near to his anticipated retirement date i.e. within 5 years of retirement, because the difference between cost of living increases and anticipated increases in earnings has less cumulative effect over this shorter period.

5.11   Where the Tribunal finds as a fact that the employment would have terminated in any event within a period of up to a year it would not be appropriate to order any compensation for loss of accrued pension rights.

(b) The Government Actuary's New Tables

5.12   Where the Applicant had 5 years or more to retirement we recommend a different approach. The Government Actuary has put forward a revised and simplified actuarial method which is described in Appendix 2 and which uses the four Tables of multipliers in Appendix 4. Public and private sector schemes attract different tables because the former usually provide a pension of $1/80^{th}$ final salary plus a lump sum, whereas the latter usually provide $1/60^{th}$ final salary with the option of partial commutation. There are also often differences between public and private sector schemes in the increases awarded to pensions in payment and the treatment of revaluation of pensions in deferment.

5.13   The approach is similar to that in the 1980 and 1991 Editions. It takes as the starting point the deferred pension to which the applicant is entitled (without any allowance for anticipated cost of living increases or other benefits) and then applies a multiplier based on the applicant's age. The figure resulting from this calculation is the starting point for working out the award for loss of enhancement of accrued benefit rights.

5.14   To calculate this figure, therefore, all that is needed is the deferred annual pension (which is usually to be found in the pension information document sent by employers to early leavers), the applicant's age and either the scheme retirement age or any earlier retirement age found by the tribunal. It is entirely an arithmetical calculation. The table assumes that the

Applicant would not have left his or her employment before retirement for reasons other than death or disability.

5.15   The figure obtained by applying the multiplier should be reduced if appropriate by a percentage representing the likelihood that the applicant would have lost his job before retirement for reasons other than unfair dismissal or discrimination, such as a fair dismissal, redundancy, leaving voluntarily etc. The 1980 paper set out a table of such deductions called the "withdrawal factor", but, as stated in the previous guidelines, we remain of the view that any such figures are inappropriate and that it is best to leave this percentage to the discretion of the Tribunal

5.16   The rationale of this scheme is that the amount a person will lose over the years can be seen as a proportion of the value of his pension and can be related to his age. Generally the younger he is the greater the loss.

5.17   Because of the simplification on which we have insisted, Tables 1 to 4 of Appendix 4 make various assumptions. They are that:

(1)   private sector pensions are based on a defined amount of pension (usually $1/60^{th}$ of final salary) of which part can be commuted to a lump sum. Public sector pensions have a lump sum payable in addition to the pension – at an amount equal to three years of pension payments at the initial rate.

(2)   there is a widow or widower's pension at 50% of the member's rate.

(3)   the maximum possible amount of pension is commuted for a lump sum.

(4)   pensions after retirement are increased annually in line with the Retail Price Index (subject to an annual limit of 5% pa for private sector scheme pensions).

(5)   no allowance has been made for the effects of contracting out.

5.18   The effects of inflation and taxation have been taken into account in the assumptions used in those tables, with particular regard to the assumed net rates of return and the allowance for a tax free lump sum, either as of right in public sector schemes or through commutation of part of the pension in private sector schemes. The actuarial basis is set out in Appendix 2 principally for the benefit of any expert who may be instructed in an individual case.

5.19   Assumptions of this nature are the only way in which the kind of simple tables set out in Appendix 4 can be put into effect. However, the assumptions are liable to change over time and we feel that the tables and the assumptions on which they are based should be reviewed periodically.

5.20   We have come to the conclusion that despite these crude assumptions it is the best system that can be devised in the circumstances. We therefore recommend it for use. If either party considers that it is inapplicable in any particular case he can put forward his arguments. The point is that it provides a starting point which can be used in the absence of more detailed evidence and modified as necessary.

5.21   Readers must note that the calculation in this section is not needed if *the substantial loss approach* described in section 8 is used to calculate future pension loss. The methodology and factors which apply to that section already allow for loss of enhancement (cf 8.3).

6. *The simplified approach* (2) – loss of pension rights from the date of dismissal to the date of hearing

6.1 Had the applicant remained in employment between the date of his dismissal and the hearing he would have gained the right to additional pension benefits. Equally he would have made additional contributions to the pension fund and his employer might well have also made contributions to the pension fund because of his continued employment.

6.2 In the case of a money purchase scheme it is usually easy to calculate the money value of the additional benefits he would have received in respect of the employer's contributions. In a final salary scheme this is not possible. Had he remained in the scheme until the date of the hearing and then left he would have qualified for a slightly higher deferred pension, but had he still been in employment at the date of the hearing then he would simply have gained additional service to put into the calculation of his final pension.

6.3 We consider that the simplest method, though not technically correct, is to look not at the additional contingent benefits he would have gained, but at the contributions which his employer would have made to the pension fund. If this is done it is not necessary to consider refinements such as widows' benefits or inflation-proofing after retirement, since the better the scheme the more money will have to go into it.

6.4 When calculating loss of earnings during this period it is necessary to work out the weekly loss and multiply it by the number of weeks between the applicant's dismissal and the hearing (allowing for any sums paid in lieu of notice). Our recommendation for calculating the loss of pension rights during this period, where there is no Recoupment, is simply to include with the weekly loss a sum to represent what the employer would have contributed notionally towards the applicant's pension had he still been employed. Of course, in the case of a final salary scheme this is not strictly a correct method of assessing the applicant's loss, since the benefit that would have accrued to the applicant by remaining in employment does not necessarily correspond to this figure, but it would, we believe, be regarded as just and equitable by both applicants and respondents.

6.5   In a typical final salary pension scheme the employer does not make a specific contribution to each person's pension, but makes a contribution to the general pension fund which is a percentage of the total wages bill or of some part of the wages bill, such as basic wages excluding commission and/or overtime. The proportion of such overall payments which is attributable to an individual employee increases with age. While in a simple case it may be felt that it is unnecessary to try to allow for this, not to do so can make a difference of as much as 25% to the multiplicand. Accordingly, tribunals should apply the factors in Tables 1 and 2 of Appendix 7 (see the example at section 6.7).

6.6   If the percentage contributed by the employer is currently anomalous (e.g. because of a "contributions holiday"), care should be taken to use the true "standard rate of contribution". This should be available in the report and accounts of the pension scheme or in the statement of pension costs for inclusion in the accounts of the employer.

6.7   If the percentage contributed by the employer cannot easily be ascertained, assume that the figure is 15% (or 20% for a non-contributory scheme) of pensionable pay. Whether a scheme is contributory or not can usually be determined by inspection of a wages slip. In each case the percentage for the employer's contribution should be multiplied by the factor from the Tables in Appendix 7 relating to the age of the employee at the date of dismissal. Applying the resulting percentage to the applicant's gross pensionable pay is, in our view, the fairest and simplest way of calculating his continuing loss of pension rights.

Example:

A is a man aged 35 and earns £300 a week gross, which is his pensionable pay. He contributes £15.00 a week (5%) to the pension fund. His employers contribute 15%

of the gross wage bill to the pension fund. His normal retirement age is 65. The factor from Table 1 of Appendix 7 is 0.88, so that A's continuing loss of pension rights is £300 x 0.15 x 0.88 = £39.60 a week.

6.8   Although to this extent pension provision is being treated as part of the applicant's weekly loss, it is not part of his wages and the Recoupment Regulations do not apply to the pension element. Thus where there is Recoupment, the pension loss element should be calculated separately.

6.9   Where there is a company money purchase scheme or where the employer is contributing to a personalised plan or a money purchase top up then assessing the contribution that the employer would have made is both the simplest and the most accurate way of assessing the employee's loss. The same system, therefore, can be applied using the percentage contributed by the employer towards the pension on a weekly basis, but without the need to apply any adjustment using the Tables in Appendix 7.

6.10 Again, readers must note that the calculation in this section is not necessary if *the substantial loss approach* described in section 8 is used to calculate future pension loss.

7. *The simplified approach* (3) – loss of future pension rights from the date of hearing

7.1   This is essentially the same as the approach to assessing loss for the period between dismissal and hearing. It may be used where the period of loss of future earnings is not likely to be more than two years. In such cases, the tribunal is making a finding which subsequent events may prove entirely incorrect, particularly where the applicant is in white-collar employment. For the applicant may find himself in a new job at a lower level with none of the prospects he had with his former employment. He may also find himself in a job which, though otherwise comparable, has no pension scheme other than a stakeholder scheme to which the employer does not contribute. Nevertheless if the tribunal decides that, when the applicant finds employment, it will be either with a comparable pension scheme or at a higher salary to offset the absence of such a scheme, the loss of future pension rights can be assessed by *the simplified approach*.

7.2   Where the pension is a money purchase scheme, the value of the loss during the fixed period is essentially the aggregate of the contributions which the employer would have made to the scheme during this period, bearing in mind that they are not taxable. Care must be taken, however, following the judgment of the Court of Appeal in **Bentwood Bros (Manchester) Ltd –v– Shepherd 2003 IRLR 364** to make allowance for accelerated payment by using, for example, Ogden Table 38. Where the pension is a final salary scheme, the loss is represented by the aggregate of contributions which the employer would have made to the pension fund during this period but subject to the same caveat.

7.3   The two qualifications to a final salary scheme calculation are:

- The employer may be taking a contributions holiday. In this case there will usually be a standard rate of contribution disclosed by the scheme and this should form the basis of the calculation.

- As discussed in section 6.5, the contributions made in respect of younger employees are used to balance out the contributions for older employees. Table 1 or 2 of Appendix 7 should be used to make any necessary adjustment. Thus the value of the lost pension rights is the contributions which would have been paid by the employer, adjusted to allow for age.

7.4   Again this calculation does not apply where *the substantial loss approach* is used.

7.5   All the above relates to occupational pension schemes but, as explained at section 2.14, if the applicant was not in a pension scheme in the lost job or is in a scheme which is not contracted out, he may still suffer a loss owing to his future S2P not accruing. Then it may be appropriate to make an award for loss of S2P accrual by using Table 3.2 in Appendix 3. This is done by taking the applicant's age at dismissal, his or her sex and gross annual earnings and reading off the percentage at those coordinates. Small adjustments to the percentage can be made to reflect actual ages and earnings. That percentage applied to annual gross earnings reflects one year's accrual of S2P which should then be multiplied by the estimated numbers of years of loss.

8. *The substantial loss approach*

8.1   We have set out in Chapter 4 the factors which the tribunal should take into account in deciding whether to use *the simplified approach* or *the substantial loss approach*. Once a decision is made to take *the substantial loss approach* the calculation is not as complex as it might at first appear.

8.2   In such cases the value of the loss of pension rights can be calculated using factors similar to those available in the Ogden Tables for personal injury and fatal accident cases. Those tables are used to calculate future loss of earnings whereas the tables in this booklet use some different assumptions (see Appendix 2). This method will be reasonably accurate either if the employee is thought unlikely to find alternative employment or when the dismissed employee has already obtained pensionable employment in a final salary or defined benefit scheme when it is possible to value the difference in benefits between the former pension scheme and the new pension scheme.

8.3   The calculation required is:

Loss of future pension rights = A minus B minus C where:

A = value of prospective final salary pension rights up to normal retirement age in former employment (if he or she had not been dismissed)

B = value of accrued final salary pension rights to date of dismissal from former employment

C = value of prospective final salary pension rights to normal retirement age in new employment

C will of course be zero if it is found that the applicant will probably not obtain further pensionable employment or if he or she has joined a money purchase scheme in the new employment. In that case, see 8.11 below.

8.4   Once these figures have been calculated, the tribunal has a further decision to make as to the amounts of any withdrawal factors. The Tables work on the basis that the applicant would have remained in his previous employment until retirement, subject to the usual risks of mortality and disability. However, it is recognised that people leave even the most stable employment for a variety of reasons. As with the Ogden Tables, no Tables are available to assist the tribunal in making this deduction. It will vary with the age, status, work record and health of the applicant and with the perceived future viability of the respondent's business.

8.5   In the case of A and B the annual amount of pension (and separate retirement lump sum where applicable, principally from public service pension schemes) is calculated on the basis of the pensionable earnings in the year up to the date of dismissal (or according to the rules of the scheme). The period of service in B is up to the date of dismissal, whereas for A the period of service is from the beginning of the employment to the individual's normal retirement age in that employment. In the case of C the annual amount of pension (and separate lump sum where applicable) is calculated on the basis of the current pensionable pay in the new employment (or the deemed pensionable pay in any assumed future employment). The period of service in C is from the date of taking up the new post to the normal retirement age in the new employment.

8.6   In each case the annual amount of pension is calculated according to the rules of the scheme, so that the annual amount of pension = pension fraction ($1/60^{th}$ or $1/80^{th}$ for example) x relevant period of service x pensionable salary. As explained above, in private sector defined benefit schemes the scheme pension fraction will often be $1/60^{th}$, with no separately identified lump sum but with the option of partial commutation. In most of the large public sector schemes the scheme pension fraction is $1/80^{th}$ and there is a separately identified lump sum equivalent to 3 times the annual amount of pension. The tables in Appendices 5 and 6 are based on these distinctions and, in the case of the private sector tables, assume commutation of pension at retirement to the maximum extent permitted. In order to simplify the calculations, guaranteed minimum pension rights are ignored. As described in Appendix 3, in certain circumstances members of contracted-out pension arrangements will be entitled to receive a 'top up pension' paid by the State from state pension age. These amounts are generally small and in the interests of simplifying the calculations this top-up pension is ignored in the calculations.

8.7   The lump sum value of A and C is found by multiplying the respective annual amounts by the factors from Tables 1 to 4 of Appendix 5 corresponding to the age of the individual. The lump sum value of B is found in the same way by using the factors from Tables 1 to 4 of Appendix 6. In the case of A and B the relevant age is at the date of dismissal. In the case of C the relevant age is at the date of commencing the new job.

8.8   Example:

A female employee is dismissed in 2002–03 at age 40 from private sector employment, which had a contracted-out pension scheme offering a pension of $1/60^{th}$ of final year's salary per year of service. Her pensionable pay in the year before she was dismissed was £20,000. She had completed 15 years of service before being dismissed and had a pensionable age of 65.

She is employed again one year later, at age 41, in a public sector job, with a salary of £15,000 and a contracted-out pension scheme offering a pension of $1/80^{th}$ of final year's salary per year of service and a lump sum of 3 years' pension, payable at normal retirement age of 60.

For the calculation of A:
Pension expected at normal retirement age in former employment
= $1/60^{th}$ x 40 (i.e. 15 years' service + 25 years to retirement) x 20,000
= £13,333.33 a year

For the calculation of B:
Pension expected at normal retirement age in former employment with service cut short at date of dismissal
= £ $1/60^{th}$ x 15 x 20,000
= £ 5,000.00 a year

For the calculation of C:
Pension expected at normal retirement age in new employment = $1/80^{th}$ x 19 x 15,000= £ 3,562.50 a year

In addition, as a matter of fact there is an expected lump sum at normal retirement age of three years' pension, namely £10,687.50, but no separate calculation is required for the lump sum in C as this is incorporated within the factors for public sector schemes. The pension schemes in both employments are contracted-out. All amounts are calculated in current terms, that is to say there is no specific allowance made for inflation, future career progression and so on, since these factors are taken into account in the multiplier factors to be applied.

Factor for the calculation of the value of A = 11.45 from Table 5.3
Factor for the calculation of the value of B = 7.56 from Table 6.3
Factor for the calculation of the value of C = 17.54 from Table 5.4

Loss of pension rights
Pension amount x factor for A (£13,333.33 x 11.45)   = £152,667
Pension amount x factor for B (£5,000.00 x 7.56)   = £ 37,800
Pension amount x factor for C (£3,562.50 x 17.54)   = £ 62,486
Loss   = £ 52,381

8.9   The blanket percentage chance or withdrawal factor, derived from **Clancy –v– Cannock Chase Technical College [2001] IRLR33**, applies to future loss of earnings. The Government Actuary, however, has argued that a blanket withdrawal factor is wrong in principle because the tribunal might have material upon which to decide, for example, that the chance of the applicant losing his new job before retirement was not as great as that of losing the old job before retirement. If the tribunal is persuaded to adopt that approach, then care must be taken to apply separate withdrawal factors to A and B on the one hand and C on the other. Accordingly, taking the example in 8.8 above and assuming the tribunal determines a 40% withdrawal factor for the lost job and a 25% withdrawal factor for the new job, the calculation will look like this:

A = £13,333.33 x 11.45 x 60%   = £91,600
B = £5,000.00 x 7.56 x 60%   = £22,680
C = £3,562.50 x 17.54 x 75%   = £46,865
Loss   = £22,055

8.10   Where the pension scheme in the previous job is a contributory scheme, allowance must be made for the fact that the applicant no longer has to pay his own contributions to the scheme. The most accurate method is to devise another table relating to such contributions. However, to simplify the calculations we suggest that this be allowed for by treating his earnings in his old employment as reduced accordingly. Thus, in calculating compensation for loss of earnings (as opposed to pension loss), any employee contributions need to be taken off the net earnings before applying the appropriate multiplier. Payslips normally show net earnings after all deductions including employee pension contributions. Similarly, if the pension scheme with the new employment is a contributory final salary scheme, the value assessed at C includes the value of the employee's contributions and hence the value of the net earnings in the new job should also be reduced accordingly.

8.11   If the applicant loses a job with a final salary pension scheme and obtains one with a money purchase scheme or signs up to a stakeholder pension, the loss is calculated as in 8.3 but only A minus B. There is no need to worry about any loss of employer pension contributions in the new job because those contributions have already been factored into the A minus B calculation. When assessing loss of earnings, however, it will be appropriate to take account of any employer contributions in the new job in order to ascertain whether there is a continuing loss of earnings or not. Thus the comparison will be the difference between net earnings in the old job (ignoring employer payroll contributions) and net earnings plus any employer pension contributions in the new.

8.12   If the applicant obtains a new job in which S2P accrues, then its value should be deducted from the value of A minus B. The value of the future accrual of S2P can be assessed using Table 3.2 in Appendix 3 based on earnings in the new employment.

Example:

As in 8.8 but instead of obtaining a public sector job, she finds work in the private sector with no pension scheme and no prospect of one. She has made no personal pension arrangements but pays her National Insurance contribution at the full rate so as to entitle her to S2P. Age at date of re-employment is 41 and her state retirement age is 65 – as she was born after 1955 (see Table 3.2). Thus:

A minus B as before but also minus C calculated in accordance with Appendix 3
£15,000 X 5.0% (extrapolated from 4.8% rising to 5.6% between 40 and 45) X 24
= £18,000.

Loss = £152,667 minus £37,800 minus £18,000 = £96,867
The result will be a smaller award if withdrawal factors are applied.

8.13   Although not strictly within *the substantial loss approach* but for the sake of completeness, if the applicant loses a job with a money purchase scheme to which the employer contributed and finds a lower paid job with no such pension scheme, the employer's contributions should be added to the continuing loss of earnings before applying the appropriate multiplier in the Ogden Tables. Any accrued S2P will have to be deducted from the result as in the above example. The use of Ogden Tables will only be appropriate where the Tribunal has decided that the loss is long term. If it is not, then *the simplified approach* in sections 6 and 7 will be used.

8.14   It should be emphasized that *the substantial loss approach* automatically includes compensation for loss of enhancement of accrued pension rights at the date of dismissal (section 5) and for loss of pension rights from the date of dismissal to the date of hearing (section 6) as well as the loss of future pension rights from the date of the hearing (section 7). Thus no further compensation needs to be added to the value derived from this approach.

9. General Conclusions

9.1   It is important to note that where the compensation exceeds the statutory limit even without consideration of loss of pension rights, the need to calculate the sum involved may remain. For it must be remembered that the Recoupment Regulations (r. 4(2)) provide for a proportionate reduction of the sum repayable to the Benefits Agency where the statutory limit applies.

9.2   Appendix 1 sets out a simple checklist for parties and tribunals to use. Appendix 2 is the Government Actuary's paper on which our conclusions as to loss of enhancement of accrued pension rights are based and also sets out the assumptions underlying the other tables. It is there primarily for the benefit of any actuarial expert who may wish to challenge the assumptions on the facts of a particular case. Appendix 3 contains a description of the State Earnings-related Pension Scheme and State Second Pension and the table for assessing the loss or future accrual of State Second Pension rights. Appendix 4 contains the tables of multipliers for assessing the loss of enhancement on accrued pension rights. Appendix 5 contains the tables of multipliers for assessing the loss of future pension rights in the lost job and Appendix 6 in the new job, using *the substantial loss approach*. Appendix 7 gives tables of factors to be applied to the contribution rates in respect of defined benefit schemes in assessing the loss of pension rights between the date of dismissal and the date of hearing and the loss of future pension rights using *the simplified approach*.

Prepared by
David Sneath   Regional Chairman Leeds
Colin Sara   Full time Chairman Bristol
Chris Daykin   Government Actuary
Adrian Gallop   Actuary, Government Actuary's Department

Appendix 1
Check list for assessing pension loss

1. Was the applicant a member of any personal or occupational pension scheme at the date of dismissal?

2. If not, is it necessary to award compensation for loss of S2P rights? See section 7.5 and Appendix 3.

3. If the applicant was a member of a personal pension scheme, did the respondent contribute to it? If so, see sections 6, 7 and 8.13.

4. If the applicant was a member of an occupational scheme, do the circumstances call for use of *the simplified approach*? See section 4. If so, see sections 5, 6 and 7.

5. If not, do the circumstances call for use of *the substantial loss approach*? If so, see section 8.

6. If the scheme was not contracted out, is it necessary to award compensation for loss of both occupational pension and S2P? See sections 7.5 and 8 and Appendix 3.

Appendix 2
Memorandum by the Government Actuary Assessing loss of occupational pension scheme rights following a finding of unfair dismissal or discrimination by an employment tribunal

Background

The 1980 paper under the above title produced by the Government Actuary's Department provided chairmen of Industrial Tribunals with a simple system of assessing the loss in respect of service before dismissal by calculating the difference between the value of the deferred pension to which the applicant remained entitled and what he would have received had he not been dismissed. The formula became less satisfactory over time because of legislative changes aimed at preserving at least some of the pension entitlement of early leavers; very approximate adjustments for this were proposed in notes issued in 1980 and 1987.

A revised system was put forward in 1989, at the time of the compilation of the first edition of the Industrial Tribunals Booklet on compensation for loss of pension rights, to take account of the legislation, together with an approximate simple formula which might be useful to chairmen in the absence of expert evidence. The formula related to a pension derived from final salary at exit, continuing (at one-half rate) to a dependant.

If a member of a final-salary pension scheme withdraws, he loses potential benefits in respect of his past service to the extent that the accrued benefits are not fully indexed in line with salaries (including an allowance for possible future promotion) until normal retirement age.

The value of each pension unit depends on many factors, in particular:

- sex, attained age, normal retirement age

- estimates of future rates of salary progression and promotion, of inflation (prices and/or pensions) and of interest on investments

- estimates of rates of withdrawal (dismissal, redundancy, resignation, transfer), death (in service and after retirement), retirement (age and ill-health) and (for dependants' benefits) age and death rates of dependants and the proportion of staff leaving an eligible dependant on their own death.

Tables were constructed for the 1989 edition and were subsequently revised for the second edition, issued in 1991. For the second edition, the tables were constructed on simplified assumptions. The method used required each pension to be divided into three parts, namely the continuing benefit value, pre- and post-1988 guaranteed minimum pension (GMP) and any balance above the GMP; a different factor was applied to each part. Tables were provided in the booklet.

To simplify procedures, a single factor was found (varying with age) to apply to the accrued pension to estimate the loss of pension rights assuming:

(i) the accrued pension for past service equalled that preserved on dismissal;

(ii) the GMP represented two-thirds of the total pension and would be revalued at least to the same extent as any balance.

It was noted these fractions would change with time.

All estimates of loss needed to be reduced by an individual assessment of the likelihood of withdrawal from the pension fund other than on account of unfair dismissal.

Loss of enhancement of accrued pension rights

One possible method to value benefit loss is to deduct the transfer value from a standard table of continuing benefit values. This methodology was considered for use in the 1991 edition of the Booklet. However, transfer values of pension rights are calculated on different assumptions from those used in valuing benefits to continuing staff. A transfer value passes between pension schemes in cash form, so the transferring scheme has to realize assets at current market rates, not the long-term average assessment. Further, there is a change in benefit expectations: the salary linkage is broken, and there are often differences in death and ill-health benefits between schemes (especially enhancement on early exit). Consequently it can be inequitable to value benefit loss by this method and it was felt to be fairer to use a table representing the loss of benefit on dismissal allowing for standard deferred benefits valued on a specified basis. This approach is still valid and it is used in this edition of the tables.

Tables 1 to 4 of Appendix 4 give factors to be applied to the amount of accrued pension at the date of dismissal to value the loss of enhancement. The approach is to value the accrued pension had it continued to increase in line with earnings until retirement age and deduct the value assuming the accrued pension increases in line with statutory revaluations (or in line with price inflation in the case of public sector schemes) until retirement age. The bases used for valuing these are set out below.

As described in Chapter 2, GMPs no longer accrue in respect of service since April 1997: thus this element will become a decreasing proportion of the pension in future. The presence of GMPs complicates the calculations and can only be allowed for in a very approximate way which will not be correct for the majority of cases. Also, GMPs did not accrue in respect of schemes which were not contracted out of SERPS. Given the preceding considerations and the Working Party's desire that any methodology adopted should be comprehensible and relatively simple to apply, it is proposed that the calculations for this edition should make no direct allowance for the effects of GMPs.

Financial assumptions
The assumptions underlying the calculations have also been reviewed in the light of changes in the demographic and economic outlook. The new calculations assume that money could be invested to earn an average of $6\frac{1}{2}\%$ per annum. For continuing benefits, based on final salary with a half-

rate pension continuing to a dependent spouse, salary is assumed to increase at 5% per annum. However, in valuing pension benefits, it is the assumptions as to the rate of return net of increases in earnings, net of increases in pensions in deferment and net of increases in pensions in payment which are important, rather than the absolute values of the assumed rates of increase.

The assumptions made for increases in pensions both in deferment and in payment are slightly different for private sector and public sector schemes to allow for the different practices in granting such increases. The level of guaranteed increases in pensions in payment varies between schemes within the private sector but must be at least equivalent to a statutory minimum for pensions accrued in respect of service since 5 April 1997 of increasing annually in line with the increase in the Retail Price Index, subject to an upper limit of 5% per annum. This statutory minimum is assumed for the increase in pensions in payment from private sector schemes. Pensions in payment from most public sector schemes increase in line with the increase in the Retail Price Index, with no upper limit. This assumption has been adopted for public sector schemes.

Frozen (deferred) benefits provided by private sector schemes are assumed to increase from the time of deferment to the time the benefit comes into payment at the lower of the increase in the Retail Price Index over that period and 5% per annum over the same period. This is equivalent to the statutory minimum increase of pensions in deferment. Frozen (deferred) benefits provided by public sector schemes are assumed to increase from the time of deferment to the time the benefit comes into payment by the increase in the Retail Price Index over that period, with no upper limit, in line with the revaluation provided by most public sector schemes.

Awards made by Employment Tribunals for loss of pension rights are tax free; however, tax is payable on the income and gains arising through any investment of the award, although it may be possible to defray the extent of this by investing in suitable tax efficient vehicles. After discussion with the ET chairmen on the working party, it was agreed that some allowance for the possible effects of tax being payable on the proceeds arising from investment of the compensation award should be made in determining the financial assumptions to be used for the rates of return net of earnings and net of revaluation of deferred pension.

It was the intention of the working party that the methodology for assessing loss of pension rights should be brought more into line with the approach used for assessing damage awards in court cases involving personal injury where heads of claim are multiplied by an appropriate multiplier, based on those given in the Ogden Tables. However, some differences remain. For instance, certain awards for loss of pension rights made by Employment Tribunals often incorporate an allowance for future increases in earnings. In general, earnings have risen on average at a faster rate than prices; it is this difference that mainly gives rise to a loss of enhancement on accrued pension rights at the date of dismissal. Awards made using the Ogden Tables approach make no allowance for any difference in the future rates of increase in earnings and prices; a rate of return net of prices rather than net of earnings is used to value earnings loss. In June 2001 the Lord Chancellor, having regard to the then recent experience of yields available on UK index-linked gilts and other considerations, specified a rate of discount of $2\frac{1}{2}\%$ per annum to be used in court cases involving damages for personal injury and fatal accidents. This yield was net of tax at the standard rate and is used for discounting future earnings, costs of care and other monetary amounts.

Having regard to the discount rate of $2\frac{1}{2}\%$, net of standard rate tax, prescribed by the Lord Chancellor for use in court cases involving personal injury, discount rates used for various purposes in the public sector, the yields available on index-linked gilts in recent years and likely future movements in these yields and the effects of tax during the roll-up period, the following financial assumptions have been made in the calculations as summarised in the following table:

Assumption	Private sector	Public sector
Gross yield	6.5%	6.5%
Yield net of earnings	1.0%	1.0%
Yield net of revaluation of deferred pensions	2.75%	2.5%
Yield net of increases in pensions in payment	3.5%	3.0%

These assumptions are not fully market-related, as they are only expected to be changed relatively infrequently.

A higher rate of statutory revaluation for pensions in deferment than for pensions in payment is assumed for private sector schemes because the revaluation in deferment is cumulative, rather than being lost if RPI exceeds 5% in a given revaluation year. Hence, the yield net of increases in deferment is lower than the yield net of increases of pensions in payment. Also a larger part of the past service benefit is statutorily subject to this revaluation than is subject to LPI in payment.

Demographic and other assumptions

The Continuous Mortality Investigation Bureau (CMIB) set up by the actuarial profession in the United Kingdom publishes tables of mortality rates derived from data relating to people who are members of insured pension schemes. The mortality rates used in the calculations have been taken as those assumed by age and gender for the calendar year 2010 in the PMA/PFA92 tables (the latest tables on insured pensioner mortality issued by the CMIB). Ill-health retirement benefits are assumed to be worth as much as those on normal retirement. No allowance is made for exits except by death; chairmen are expected to assess for themselves the reduction for the possibility of withdrawal (by resignation etc. but not unfair dismissal) before normal pension age. In valuing the pension benefits, it is assumed that the member would be married at death and that the spouse would be entitled to a pension of half that payable to the member in the case of death after retirement or death in deferment or which would have been payable to the member based on potential service to normal retirement age at the date of death in the case of death in service.

No allowance has been made for expenses of any kind which might be incurred by the individual were he or she to purchase pension benefits equivalent to those lost.

The factors in the tables in Appendices 4, 5 and 6 also make allowance for the availability of a tax free lump sum; either, for private sector schemes, by commutation to the maximum extent permitted or, in the case of public sector schemes, by inclusion of the benefit of a lump sum of three times the annual pension paid at the date of retirement. The lump sum amounts have been grossed up within the total figures, so that the whole amount can be regarded as the equivalent taxable payment.

Loss of future pension rights

Simplified approach

The 1991 edition of the booklet assessed the loss of future pension rights by assuming that the loss was equivalent in value to the contributions that the employer would have made to the pension scheme in respect of the employee's employment. *The simplified approach* discussed in Chapters 4 to 7 of the booklet follows this approach. However, as discussed in paragraph 6.5 of the booklet, in a typical final salary pension scheme the employer does not make a specific contribution to each person's pension, but makes a contribution to the general pension fund which is a proportion of the total wages bill or of some part of the wages bill. To make some allowance for the fact that the accrual of pension in respect of a year's pensionable service usually increases with age, whereas the employer is paying an aggregate contribution in respect of all members of the scheme and which does not usually vary by age, the overall percentage contribution payable by the employer should be multiplied by a factor related to the employee's age at the date of dismissal. These factors are set out in Tables 1 and 2 of Appendix 7. These have been obtained by calculating the value of the pension earned through one year of pensionable service at each year of age from age 20 onwards until the assumed retirement age, allowing for increases in salary before retirement but with no allowance made for exit from the scheme before the scheme retirement age is reached other than death. The average of the resulting contribution rates is then taken. The figure given for a particular age in the tables is the ratio of the assessed contribution rate for that age divided by the average contribution rate.

Substantial loss approach

This approach does not use future contributions that would have been made to the pension scheme to assess the value of future pension rights. Instead, the value of the pension benefits up to normal retirement age which would have been earned had the employee not been dismissed is determined. From this is deducted the value of the accrued pension rights at the date of dismissal and the value of any prospective pension rights arising from any new employment since dismissal. The various values required are assessed by multiplying the accrued or estimated total pension by appropriate multipliers. This approach is akin to that used for assessing damages awards in personal injury cases and uses factors similar to those given in the Ogden Tables. These factors are given in tables in Appendices 5 and 6. The methodology, termed *the substantial loss approach*, is discussed in more detail in Chapter 8. The factors have been calculated using the same financial and demographic assumptions as those used in the simplified loss approach for calculating loss of enhancement of accrued pension rights.

Loss of accrual of future state second pension rights

The various types of pension benefit provided by the State are discussed in Chapter 2. It is proposed there that it be assumed there is no loss of accrual of Basic State Pension but that the loss of any State Second Pension (S2P) should be compensated.

S2P is essentially an earnings-related benefit under which tranches of earnings between various lower and upper limits in any tax year are revalued in line with the general increase in earnings until the year preceding that in which state pension age is attained. These revalued earnings are then averaged over the period from age 16, or April 1978, if later, to the end of the year preceding state pension age. The resulting pension is payable from state pension age and is indexed in line with the general level of prices.

Under the State Earnings-Related Pension Scheme (SERPS), the accrual rate depended on the year in which state pension age was attained; for those retiring up to April 2009 there was a phased reduction in the accrual rate from $25/N$ to $20/N$ where N is the number of tax years in the earner's working life from April 1978 to the end of the year preceding state pension age. Under the changes initiated by the Child Support, Pensions and Social Security Act 2000, SERPS was reformed into S2P. These reforms introduced the different accrual rates on different bands of earnings that are double, half and equal to the previous SERPS accrual rates.

Given assumptions about future increases in the general levels of earnings, the amount of the S2P benefits which would arise from state pension age in respect of earnings in a particular tax year can be estimated. This accrued S2P would not then alter regardless of whether the person remained in employment in the future or not. Given assumptions about the rate of state pension increases, the discount yield and future mortality rates, a value can be assigned to £1 of earnings accrued in each of the three various bands in a given year.

Table 3.2 in Appendix 3 show the values of the S2P pension arising from £1 of gross earnings, calculated using the financial and demographic assumptions used to value the loss of pension rights from occupational and other pension arrangements, described earlier in this Appendix, together with other demographic assumptions used in the calculations of contracting-out rebates in the report *Review of certain contracting-out terms* (Cm 5076).

If it is assumed that the claimant's earnings in his old employment would have increased in line with the earnings revaluations applied to the accrual of S2P then an estimate of the S2P accrued over a given number of years can be found by multiplying the gross earnings by the appropriate factors given in Table 3.2 in Appendix 3 and then by the number of years over which S2P is assumed to accrue. The value of any S2P accrued in any new employment can be assessed in the same way.

General

It should be noted that the basis used for assessing the loss of pension rights is intended to provide a just and equitable level of compensation to individuals found to have been wrongly dismissed for whatever reason, taking into account the interests of all the parties involved. It does not necessarily correspond to actuarial funding bases used by pension schemes in general.

The tables of factors in Appendix 4 are for use in calculating the loss of enhancement on accrued pension rights, as discussed in Chapter 5. The tables in Appendices 5 and 6 are for use in cases assessing the loss of future pension rights using *the substantial loss approach*, described in Section 8. The factors in Appendix 7 are those to be applied to the overall contribution rate to the scheme to estimate the appropriate age specific contribution rates.

Where the value of scheme benefits is not known, it is suggested that an average (sixtieths) scheme should be assumed with a standard contribution rate taken as 20% of pensionable salary, then multiplied by a factor from Appendix 7, as appropriate. It must be emphasized that pensionable salary may not be the same as total salary.

Chris Daykin
Government Actuary
December 2002

Appendix 3
State Earnings-Related Pension Scheme (SERPS) and State Second Pension (S2P)

SERPS

Since April 1978, employees who have paid national insurance contributions on earnings over the lower earnings limit have been entitled to an earnings-related additional pension payable by the State and generally referred to as the State Earnings-Related Pension Scheme (SERPS). Since April 2000 employees earning between the lower earnings limit and the primary threshold for National Insurance contributions are treated as having paid the necessary NI contributions and hence qualified for SERPS accrual. Earnings between the lower earnings and upper earnings limits in any tax year ("relevant earnings") are revalued in line with the general level of increase in earnings up to the year before that in which state pension age is attained. These revalued earnings are then averaged over the period from age 16, or April 1978 if later, to the end of the year preceding state pension age. The retirement pension is payable from state pension age and is indexed after that age in line with the general level of prices.

State pension age for men is 65. State pension age is age 60 for women retiring up to 5 April 2010. For women retiring from 6 April 2020 onwards state pension age will be 65, as it is for men. Between these dates, state pension age for women will increase by one month in every two month interval as set out in Table 3.1.

Following the Social Security Contributions and Benefits Act 1992 the additional pension was eventually to be 20 per cent of revalued earnings as defined above and could be regarded as accruing uniformly over the working life between age 16 and the end of the tax year preceding state pension age. For those over 16 in April 1978 when the accrual of additional

Table 3.1 State pension age for women – adjustments

Date of birth	State pension age (year. month)	Pension date	Date of birth	State pension age (year. month)	Pension date
06.03.50	60.0	06.03.2010	06.10.52	62.7	06.05.2015
06.04.50	60.1	06.05.2010	06.11.52	62.8	06.07.2015
06.05.50	60.2	06.07.2010	06.12.52	62.9	06.09.2015
06.06.50	60.3	06.09.2010	06.01.53	62.10	06.11.2015
06.07.50	60.4	06.11.2010	06.02.53	62.11	06.01.2016
06.08.50	60.5	06.01.2011	06.03.53	63.0	06.03.2016
06.09.50	60.6	06.03.2011	06.04.53	63.1	06.05.2016
06.10.50	60.7	06.05.2011	06.05.53	63.2	06.07.2016
06.11.50	60.8	06.07.2011	06.06.53	63.3	06.09.2016
06.12.50	60.9	06.09.2011	06.07.53	63.4	06.11.2016
06.01.51	60.10	06.11.2011	06.08.53	63.5	06.01.2017
06.02.51	60.11	06.01.2012	06.09.53	63.6	06.03.2017
06.03.51	61.0	06.03.2012	06.10.53	63.7	06.05.2017
06.04.51	61.1	06.05.2012	06.11.53	63.8	06.07.2017
06.05.51	61.2	06.07.2012	06.12.53	63.9	06.09.2017
06.06.51	61.3	06.09.2012	06.01.54	63.10	06.11.2017
06.07.51	61.4	06.11.2012	06.02.54	63.11	06.01.2018
06.08.51	61.5	06.01.2013	06.03.54	64.0	06.03.2018
06.09.51	61.6	06.03.2013	06.04.54	64.1	06.05.2018
06.10.51	61.7	06.05.2013	06.05.54	64.2	06.07.2018
06.11.51	61.8	06.07.2013	06.06.54	64.3	06.09.2018
06.12.51	61.9	06.09.2013	06.07.54	64.4	06.11.2018
06.01.52	61.10	06.11.2013	06.08.54	64.5	06.01.2019
06.02.52	61.11	06.01.2014	06.09.54	64.6	06.03.2019
06.03.52	62.0	06.03.2014	06.10.54	64.7	06.05.2019
06.04.52	62.1	06.05.2014	06.11.54	64.8	06.07.2019
06.05.52	62.2	06.07.2014	06.12.54	64.9	06.09.2019
06.06.52	62.3	06.09.2014	06.01.55	64.10	06.11.2019
06.07.52	62.4	06.11.2014	06.02.55	64.11	06.01.2020
06.08.52	62.5	06.01.2015	06.03.55	65.0	06.03.2020
06.09.52	62.6	06.03.2015	06.04.55	65.0	06.04.2020

pension commenced, the working life was taken to be between April 1978 and the end of the tax year preceding state pension age.

For people reaching state pension age after April 1999, the accrual rate will be 25/N per cent in respect of earnings up to April 1988, where N is the number of tax years in the earner's working life from April 1978 or age 16, if later, to the end of the one preceding state pension age. However, the accrual rate in respect of earnings after April 1988 depends on the year in which state pension age is attained as follows:

Year of retirement	Percentage accrual rate for period 1988–89 onwards
2003–04	23/25
2004–05	22.5/26
2005–06	22/27
2006–07	21.5/28
2007–08	21/29
2008–09	20.5/30
2009–10	20/31
2010–11	20/32
....	....
2027–28 and later	20/49

The State Second Pension

The Child Support, Pensions and Social Security Act 2000 introduced a number of changes to additional pension, which is now known as The State Second Pension (S2P). The main changes, which took effect from the tax year 2002–03, were:

- The introduction of three different accrual rates on different bands of earnings

- Treating those earning between the annualized lower earnings limit (the qualifying earnings factor or QEF set to be £4,004 in 2003–04) up to the "low earnings threshold" – £11,200 in terms of 2003–04 earnings – as though they earned the low earnings threshold

- Treating qualified carers and people with long-term disabilities who have no earnings or earnings below the annual lower earnings limit, as if they had earnings at the level of the low earnings threshold.

S2P will accrue on earnings (actual or treated as earned) between the lower earnings limit and the upper earnings limit. These earnings ("relevant earnings") will initially be divided into three bands. Band 1 will be from the annual lower earnings limit to the low earnings threshold (LET). Band 2 will be from the low earnings threshold plus £1 to an amount equal to 3 x LET – 2 x QEF. This would be £25,600 in terms of 2003–04 earnings. Band 3 will be from the top of the second band plus £1 to the upper earnings limit. The lower and upper earnings limits and the low earnings threshold will be revalued from year to year.

The S2P accrual rates will be double, half and equal to the SERPS accrual rates on bands 1, 2 and 3 of earnings respectively. Thus, for example, for retirements in 2009–10 and later the S2P will be based on 40%, 10% and 20% of earnings in bands 1, 2 and 3 respectively.

Potential loss of S2P

S2P will be accrued by all employees earning over the lower earnings limit who are in pension arrangements which are not contracted-out of the S2P. Thus, for any employee who is not a member of an occupational scheme or is a member of an occupational pension scheme which was not contracted out of S2P (circumstances which currently apply to about three-quarters of the private sector working population, but to only a small proportion of public sector workers) there is a potential loss of rights in relation to S2P.

The value of the loss of future accrual of S2P can be obtained by using the relevant factor from Table 3.2 of this appendix which reflects the value of one year's accrual of S2P by age and sex. To obtain the value of the loss of S2P rights, the appropriate factor is taken from Table 3.2 according to the applicant's age at the date of dismissal and sex. The gross earnings of the applicant at the date of dismissal are then multiplied by this factor to give the value of one year's accrual of S2P. The resulting amount should then be multiplied by the length of the period, in years, for which the loss is being valued. The basis used for calculating the factors is described in Appendix 2.

Table 3.2 Factor to be applied to gross earnings for valuing loss of future accruals of S2P for one year

	QEF = 4108		LET = 11600		UEL = 31720		(2004–2005)	
	Salary							
Men (age)	**5,000**	**6,000**	**7,000**	**8,000**	**9,000**	**10,000**	**11,000**	**12,000**
20	9.6%	8.0%	6.8%	6.0%	5.3%	4.8%	4.4%	4.0%
25	10.1%	8.4%	7.2%	6.3%	5.6%	5.0%	4.6%	4.3%
30	10.6%	8.9%	7.6%	6.6%	5.9%	5.3%	4.8%	4.5%
35	11.3%	9.4%	8.1%	7.1%	6.3%	5.6%	5.1%	4.8%
40	12.0%	10.0%	8.6%	7.5%	6.7%	6.0%	5.4%	5.1%
45	13.8%	11.5%	9.8%	8.6%	7.6%	6.9%	6.3%	5.8%
50	16.5%	13.7%	11.8%	10.3%	9.2%	8.2%	7.5%	7.0%
55	20.1%	16.8%	14.4%	12.6%	11.2%	10.1%	9.2%	8.5%
60	25.5%	21.3%	18.2%	15.9%	14.2%	12.8%	11.6%	10.8%
63	31.9%	26.6%	22.8%	19.9%	17.7%	15.9%	14.5%	13.5%
Women (age)								
20	10.7%	8.9%	7.6%	6.7%	5.9%	5.3%	4.9%	4.5%
25	11.2%	9.4%	8.0%	7.0%	6.2%	5.6%	5.1%	4.7%
30	11.8%	9.9%	8.5%	7.4%	6.6%	5.9%	5.4%	5.0%
35	12.5%	10.4%	8.9%	7.8%	6.9%	6.2%	5.7%	5.3%
40	13.2%	11.0%	9.4%	8.2%	7.3%	6.6%	6.0%	5.6%
45	15.0%	12.5%	10.7%	9.4%	8.3%	7.5%	6.8%	6.3%
50	19.6%	16.3%	14.0%	12.2%	10.9%	9.8%	8.9%	8.3%
55	31.2%	26.0%	22.3%	19.5%	17.4%	15.6%	14.2%	13.2%
58	38.6%	32.2%	27.6%	24.1%	21.4%	19.3%	17.5%	16.3%

13,000	14,000	15,000	20,000	25,000	30,000	35,000	40,000	45,000	50,000
3.9%	3.7%	3.6%	3.1%	2.8%	2.8%	2.5%	2.2%	2.0%	1.8%
4.1%	3.9%	3.7%	3.2%	2.9%	2.9%	2.7%	2.3%	2.1%	1.9%
4.3%	4.1%	3.9%	3.4%	3.1%	3.1%	2.8%	2.4%	2.2%	2.0%
4.5%	4.4%	4.2%	3.6%	3.3%	3.2%	3.0%	2.6%	2.3%	2.1%
4.8%	4.6%	4.4%	3.8%	3.5%	3.4%	3.2%	2.8%	2.5%	2.2%
5.5%	5.3%	5.1%	4.4%	4.0%	4.0%	3.6%	3.2%	2.8%	2.5%
6.6%	6.4%	6.1%	5.3%	4.8%	4.7%	4.3%	3.8%	3.4%	3.0%
8.1%	7.8%	7.5%	6.4%	5.8%	5.8%	5.3%	4.6%	4.1%	3.7%
10.3%	9.8%	9.5%	8.2%	7.4%	7.3%	6.7%	5.9%	5.2%	4.7%
12.8%	12.3%	11.8%	10.2%	9.2%	9.2%	8.4%	7.3%	6.5%	5.9%
4.3%	4.1%	4.0%	3.4%	3.1%	3.1%	2.8%	2.5%	2.2%	2.0%
4.5%	4.3%	4.2%	3.6%	3.3%	3.2%	3.0%	2.6%	2.3%	2.1%
4.8%	4.6%	4.4%	3.8%	3.4%	3.4%	3.1%	2.7%	2.4%	2.2%
5.0%	4.8%	4.6%	4.0%	3.6%	3.6%	3.3%	2.9%	2.6%	2.3%
5.3%	5.1%	4.9%	4.2%	3.8%	3.8%	3.5%	3.0%	2.7%	2.4%
6.0%	5.8%	5.6%	4.8%	4.3%	4.3%	4.0%	3.5%	3.1%	2.8%
7.9%	7.5%	7.3%	6.3%	5.7%	5.6%	5.1%	4.5%	4.0%	3.6%
12.6%	12.0%	11.6%	10.0%	9.0%	9.0%	8.2%	7.2%	6.4%	5.8%
15.5%	14.9%	14.3%	12.4%	11.2%	11.1%	10.2%	8.9%	7.9%	7.1%

Example

A male employee is dismissed in 2003–04 at age 50 from private sector employment with gross earnings of £35,000 a year and no prospect of reemployment before state pension age of 65. The claimant was not a member of any pension arrangements run by the employer and hence was accruing S2P since his earnings are above the lower earnings limit. The loss for future accrual of S2P is assessed as

£35,000 x 0.043 x 15 = £22,575

where the factor of 0.043 is taken from Table 3.2 at age 50 for males with gross earnings of £35,000.

If the employee was a member of a pension arrangement which was contracted out of the Additional Pension under SERPS and/or S2P, there will be a potential loss of state pension benefits under S2P for members of employer contracted-out final salary schemes and contracted-out money purchase schemes with earnings below 3 x LET – 2 x QEF (= £25,600 in 2003–04 terms) and for employee members of Appropriate Personal Pensions with earnings below the Lower Earnings Threshold (= £11,200 in 2003–04 terms). Had the member not been dismissed, a top-up pension would have been paid by the State from the state pension age equal to the amount of S2P the member would have accrued less the amount of SERPS the member would notionally have accrued. The loss of the SERPS accrual is effectively allowed for in the assessment of the loss of occupational pension rights, as discussed in section 5 et seq. Hence, the loss of state pension benefits in respect of future service which are not allowed for elsewhere can be assessed as the value of the S2P which would have been paid in respect of future service less the value of the amount of SERPS the member would notionally have accrued. However, the value of this top-up is complex to calculate and is usually small relative to the value of the loss of pension from the pension scheme. In keeping with the aim of simplifying the calculations as far as possible, it is recommended that no award of compensation be made in respect of the potential loss of any top-up pension payable to members of contracted out pension arrangements.

There may be cases where the employee was a member of a company occupational pension scheme which was not contracted out. This means that there are two potential losses which have to be assessed separately; one under S2P and the second under the occupational pension scheme. The methods for assessing this second loss are discussed in Chapters 5, 6, 7 and 8. An employee who was not previously a member of an occupational pension scheme will not suffer a loss of future pension rights (other than those payable by the State) unless the employer was contributing to a personal pension or stakeholder pension on behalf of the employee, in which case the loss can be measured as the loss of that contribution (see Chapter 7).

In general, the lower and upper earnings limits and the lower earnings threshold will be uprated at the beginning of each tax year. Thus the figures in Table 3.2 will need to be revised on an annual basis; in calculating the value of the S2P loss on dismissal, factors relevant to the tax year in which dismissal took place should be applied to the gross earnings as at the date of dismissal.

Where the factors are used to value the S2P accruing from some future employment, the table of factors for the latest available tax year should be used and applied to the assessed gross earnings in the new employment.

Appendix 4
Tables of multipliers to be applied to the deferred annual pension to assess compensation for loss of enhancement of accrued pension rights (Chapter 5)

Table 4.1 Men in private sector schemes

Age last birthday at dismissal	Normal retirement age – men			Age last birthday at dismissal	Normal retirement age – men		
	55	60	65		55	60	65
20 and under	5.62	5.22	4.63	43	2.85	3.31	3.37
21	5.55	5.18	4.60	44	2.65	3.16	3.28
22	5.49	5.13	4.57	45	2.45	3.02	3.17
23	5.41	5.09	4.55	46	2.23	2.86	3.07
24	5.34	5.03	4.51	47	2.01	2.70	2.96
25	5.25	4.98	4.48	48	1.77	2.53	2.84
26	5.17	4.92	4.44	49	1.53	2.36	2.72
27	5.08	4.86	4.41	50	1.28	2.18	2.59
28	4.98	4.80	4.37	51	1.01	1.99	2.46
29	4.88	4.73	4.32	52	0.74	1.79	2.32
30	4.78	4.66	4.28	53	0.45	1.58	2.18
31	4.67	4.58	4.23	54	0.15	1.37	2.03
32	4.55	4.50	4.18	55		1.14	1.87
33	4.43	4.42	4.12	56		0.91	1.71
34	4.30	4.33	4.06	57		0.66	1.54
35	4.17	4.24	4.00	58		0.40	1.37
36	4.03	4.14	3.94	59		0.14	1.18
37	3.88	4.03	3.87	60			0.99
38	3.73	3.93	3.79	61			0.79
39	3.57	3.81	3.72	62			0.57
40	3.40	3.70	3.64	63			0.35
41	3.22	3.57	3.55	64			0.12
42	3.04	3.44	3.47				

Table 4.2 Men in public sector schemes

Age last birthday at dismissal	Normal retirement age – men			Age last birthday at dismissal	Normal retirement age – men		
	55	*60*	*65*		*55*	*60*	*65*
20 and under	6.26	5.91	5.33	43	3.10	3.65	3.80
21	6.19	5.85	5.30	44	2.88	3.49	3.69
22	6.10	5.80	5.26	45	2.66	3.33	3.57
23	6.02	5.74	5.22	46	2.42	3.15	3.45
24	5.92	5.68	5.18	47	2.17	2.97	3.32
25	5.83	5.61	5.14	48	1.92	2.78	3.18
26	5.73	5.54	5.09	49	1.65	2.59	3.05
27	5.62	5.47	5.05	50	1.38	2.39	2.90
28	5.51	5.39	4.99	51	1.09	2.18	2.75
29	5.39	5.31	4.94	52	0.79	1.96	2.59
30	5.27	5.22	4.88	53	0.49	1.73	2.43
31	5.14	5.13	4.82	54	0.16	1.49	2.26
32	5.01	5.04	4.76	55		1.24	2.09
33	4.87	4.94	4.69	56		0.99	1.90
34	4.72	4.83	4.62	57		0.72	1.71
35	4.57	4.72	4.54	58		0.44	1.52
36	4.41	4.61	4.47	59		0.15	1.31
37	4.25	4.49	4.38	60			1.10
38	4.08	4.36	4.30	61			0.87
39	3.90	4.23	4.21	62			0.64
40	3.71	4.10	4.11	63			0.39
41	3.51	3.96	4.01	64			0.13
42	3.31	3.81	3.91				

Table 4.3 Women in private sector schemes

Age last birthday at dismissal	Normal retirement age – women			Age last birthday at dismissal	Normal retirement age – women		
	55	*60*	*65*		*55*	*60*	*65*
20 and under	5.89	5.54	4.96	43	2.98	3.50	3.61
21	5.83	5.49	4.94	44	2.77	3.35	3.50
22	5.75	5.44	4.91	45	2.56	3.19	3.39
23	5.68	5.39	4.88	46	2.33	3.02	3.28
24	5.59	5.34	4.84	47	2.10	2.85	3.16
25	5.51	5.28	4.81	48	1.85	2.68	3.04
26	5.42	5.22	4.77	49	1.60	2.49	2.91
27	5.32	5.15	4.73	50	1.33	2.30	2.77
28	5.22	5.09	4.68	51	1.06	2.09	2.63
29	5.12	5.01	4.63	52	0.77	1.88	2.48
30	5.00	4.94	4.58	53	0.47	1.67	2.33
31	4.89	4.85	4.53	54	0.16	1.44	2.17
32	4.77	4.77	4.47	55		1.20	2.00
33	4.64	4.68	4.42	56		0.95	1.83
34	4.50	4.58	4.35	57		0.69	1.64
35	4.36	4.48	4.28	58		0.42	1.46
36	4.21	4.38	4.21	59		0.14	1.26
37	4.06	4.27	4.14	60			1.05
38	3.90	4.16	4.06	61			0.84
39	3.73	4.03	3.98	62			0.61
40	3.55	3.91	3.89	63			0.37
41	3.37	3.78	3.80	64			0.13
42	3.18	3.64	3.71				

Table 4.4 Women in public sector schemes

Age last birthday at dismissal	Normal retirement age – women			Age last birthday at dismissal	Normal retirement age – women		
	55	60	65		55	60	65
20 and under	6.53	6.22	5.68	43	3.23	3.84	4.04
21	6.45	6.17	5.65	44	3.00	3.67	3.92
22	6.36	6.11	5.61	45	2.76	3.49	3.79
23	6.27	6.04	5.57	46	2.51	3.31	3.66
24	6.18	5.98	5.52	47	2.26	3.12	3.53
25	6.08	5.91	5.48	48	1.99	2.92	3.38
26	5.97	5.83	5.43	49	1.72	2.72	3.24
27	5.86	5.75	5.38	50	1.43	2.50	3.08
28	5.74	5.67	5.32	51	1.13	2.28	2.92
29	5.62	5.59	5.26	52	0.82	2.05	2.75
30	5.49	5.49	5.20	53	0.50	1.81	2.58
31	5.36	5.40	5.14	54	0.17	1.56	2.40
32	5.22	5.30	5.07	55		1.30	2.21
33	5.07	5.19	4.99	56		1.03	2.02
34	4.92	5.08	4.92	57		0.75	1.81
35	4.76	4.97	4.84	58		0.46	1.60
36	4.59	4.85	4.75	59		0.15	1.38
37	4.42	4.72	4.66	60			1.16
38	4.24	4.59	4.57	61			0.92
39	4.05	4.45	4.48	62			0.67
40	3.86	4.31	4.37	63			0.41
41	3.66	4.16	4.27	64			0.14
42	3.44	4.00	4.16				

Appendix 5
Tables of multipliers to be applied to the estimated final annual pension to assess value of pension arising from service to Normal Retirement Age (Chapter 8)

Table 5.1 Men in private sector schemes

Age last birthday at dismissal	Normal retirement age – men			Age last birthday at dismissal	Normal retirement age – men		
	55	60	65		55	60	65
20 and under	12.79	10.83	8.91	43	16.24	13.75	11.29
21	12.92	10.94	9.00	44	16.42	13.89	11.41
22	13.05	11.05	9.09	45	16.60	14.04	11.53
23	13.19	11.16	9.18	46	16.78	14.20	11.66
24	13.32	11.28	9.27	47	16.97	14.35	11.78
25	13.46	11.39	9.36	48	17.16	14.51	11.91
26	13.60	11.51	9.46	49	17.35	14.67	12.04
27	13.74	11.63	9.56	50	17.55	14.84	12.17
28	13.88	11.75	9.66	51	17.76	15.01	12.30
29	14.02	11.87	9.76	52	17.97	15.18	12.44
30	14.17	11.99	9.86	53	18.19	15.36	12.58
31	14.32	12.12	9.96	54	18.42	15.55	12.72
32	14.47	12.25	10.07	55		15.74	12.87
33	14.62	12.37	10.17	56		15.95	13.03
34	14.77	12.50	10.28	57		16.16	13.19
35	14.93	12.64	10.39	58		16.38	13.36
36	15.08	12.77	10.50	59		16.61	13.54
37	15.24	12.90	10.61	60			13.73
38	15.40	13.04	10.72	61			13.93
39	15.57	13.18	10.83	62			14.14
40	15.73	13.32	10.95	63			14.37
41	15.90	13.46	11.06	64			14.62
42	16.07	13.60	11.18				

Table 5.2 Men in public sector schemes

Age last birthday at dismissal	Normal retirement age – men			Age last birthday at dismissal	Normal retirement age – men		
	55	*60*	*65*		*55*	*60*	*65*
20 and under	15.97	13.65	11.36	43	20.26	17.31	14.40
21	16.13	13.79	11.47	44	20.48	17.50	14.55
22	16.30	13.93	11.59	45	20.70	17.68	14.70
23	16.46	14.07	11.71	46	20.93	17.88	14.86
24	16.63	14.21	11.82	47	21.16	18.07	15.02
25	16.80	14.36	11.95	48	21.40	18.27	15.18
26	16.98	14.51	12.07	49	21.64	18.48	15.35
27	17.15	14.66	12.19	50	21.89	18.69	15.52
28	17.33	14.81	12.32	51	22.15	18.90	15.69
29	17.51	14.96	12.44	52	22.41	19.12	15.87
30	17.69	15.12	12.57	53	22.69	19.35	16.05
31	17.87	15.27	12.70	54	22.97	19.59	16.24
32	18.06	15.43	12.84	55		19.83	16.44
33	18.25	15.59	12.97	56		20.09	16.64
34	18.44	15.75	13.11	57		20.35	16.85
35	18.63	15.92	13.24	58		20.63	17.07
36	18.82	16.08	13.38	59		20.92	17.30
37	19.02	16.25	13.52	60			17.55
38	19.22	16.42	13.66	61			17.81
39	19.42	16.60	13.80	62			18.08
40	19.63	16.77	13.95	63			18.38
41	19.83	16.95	14.10	64			18.70
42	20.05	17.13	14.24				

Table 5.3 Women in private sector schemes

Age last birthday at dismissal	Normal retirement age – women			Age last birthday at dismissal	Normal retirement age – women		
	55	**60**	**65**		**55**	**60**	**65**
20 and under	13.26	11.32	9.37	43	16.74	14.28	11.81
21	13.39	11.43	9.47	44	16.92	14.43	11.93
22	13.53	11.55	9.56	45	17.10	14.58	12.05
23	13.67	11.67	9.66	46	17.28	14.73	12.18
24	13.80	11.78	9.75	47	17.47	14.89	12.30
25	13.94	11.90	9.85	48	17.66	15.05	12.43
26	14.08	12.02	9.95	49	17.85	15.21	12.56
27	14.23	12.14	10.05	50	18.05	15.38	12.70
28	14.37	12.27	10.15	51	18.25	15.55	12.84
29	14.52	12.39	10.26	52	18.46	15.72	12.98
30	14.66	12.51	10.36	53	18.67	15.90	13.12
31	14.81	12.64	10.46	54	18.89	16.08	13.27
32	14.96	12.77	10.57	55		16.27	13.42
33	15.11	12.90	10.67	56		16.47	13.58
34	15.27	13.03	10.78	57		16.67	13.74
35	15.42	13.16	10.89	58		16.88	13.91
36	15.58	13.30	11.00	59		17.10	14.09
37	15.74	13.43	11.11	60			14.27
38	15.90	13.57	11.22	61			14.46
39	16.07	13.71	11.34	62			14.66
40	16.23	13.85	11.45	63			14.88
41	16.40	13.99	11.57	64			15.10
42	16.57	14.13	11.69				

Table 5.4 Women in public sector schemes

Age last birthday at dismissal	Normal retirement age – women			Age last birthday at dismissal	Normal retirement age – women		
	55	60	65		55	60	65
20 and under	16.48	14.19	11.91	43	20.81	17.91	15.01
21	16.64	14.33	12.02	44	21.02	18.09	15.16
22	16.81	14.48	12.15	45	21.25	18.28	15.32
23	16.98	14.62	12.27	46	21.47	18.48	15.48
24	17.15	14.77	12.39	47	21.70	18.67	15.64
25	17.32	14.92	12.51	48	21.94	18.87	15.81
26	17.50	15.07	12.64	49	22.18	19.08	15.98
27	17.68	15.22	12.77	50	22.42	19.28	16.15
28	17.86	15.37	12.90	51	22.67	19.50	16.33
29	18.04	15.53	13.03	52	22.93	19.72	16.51
30	18.22	15.69	13.16	53	23.19	19.94	16.69
31	18.40	15.85	13.29	54	23.46	20.17	16.88
32	18.59	16.01	13.43	55		20.41	17.08
33	18.78	16.17	13.56	56		20.65	17.28
34	18.97	16.33	13.70	57		20.90	17.48
35	19.16	16.50	13.84	58		21.16	17.70
36	19.36	16.67	13.98	59		21.43	17.92
37	19.56	16.84	14.12	60			18.15
38	19.76	17.01	14.26	61			18.40
39	19.96	17.18	14.41	62			18.65
40	20.17	17.36	14.56	63			18.92
41	20.38	17.54	14.70	64			19.21
42	20.59	17.72	14.86				

Appendix 6
Tables of multipliers to be applied to the deferred annual pension to assess value of deferred pension (Chapter 8)

Table 6.1 Men in private sector schemes

Age last birthday at dismissal	Normal retirement age – men			Age last birthday at dismissal	Normal retirement age – men		
	55	**60**	**65**		**55**	**60**	**65**
20 and under	7.17	5.61	4.28	43	13.39	10.44	7.92
21	7.37	5.76	4.40	44	13.76	10.73	8.14
22	7.57	5.92	4.51	45	14.15	11.03	8.36
23	7.77	6.08	4.63	46	14.55	11.33	8.59
24	7.98	6.24	4.76	47	14.96	11.65	8.83
25	8.20	6.41	4.88	48	15.38	11.98	9.07
26	8.43	6.59	5.02	49	15.82	12.31	9.32
27	8.66	6.77	5.15	50	16.28	12.66	9.57
28	8.90	6.95	5.29	51	16.75	13.02	9.84
29	9.14	7.14	5.43	52	17.24	13.40	10.12
30	9.39	7.34	5.58	53	17.74	13.78	10.40
31	9.65	7.54	5.73	54	18.27	14.19	10.69
32	9.92	7.74	5.89	55		14.60	11.00
33	10.19	7.96	6.05	56		15.04	11.32
34	10.47	8.18	6.22	57		15.50	11.65
35	10.76	8.40	6.39	58		15.97	12.00
36	11.06	8.63	6.56	59		16.47	12.36
37	11.36	8.87	6.74	60			12.74
38	11.68	9.11	6.92	61			13.14
39	12.00	9.36	7.11	62			13.56
40	12.33	9.62	7.31	63			14.02
41	12.67	9.89	7.51	64			14.50
42	13.03	10.16	7.71				

Table 6.2 Men in public sector schemes

Age last birthday at dismissal	Normal retirement age – men			Age last birthday at dismissal	Normal retirement age – men		
	55	**60**	**65**		**55**	**60**	**65**
20 and under	9.71	7.74	6.03	43	17.16	13.66	10.59
21	9.95	7.93	6.18	44	17.60	14.00	10.86
22	10.19	8.13	6.33	45	18.05	14.36	11.13
23	10.45	8.33	6.48	46	18.51	14.72	11.41
24	10.71	8.54	6.64	47	18.99	15.10	11.70
25	10.97	8.75	6.81	48	19.48	15.49	12.00
26	11.25	8.97	6.97	49	19.99	15.89	12.30
27	11.53	9.19	7.15	50	20.51	16.30	12.62
28	11.82	9.42	7.32	51	21.06	16.73	12.94
29	12.11	9.65	7.50	52	21.62	17.17	13.27
30	12.42	9.89	7.69	53	22.20	17.62	13.62
31	12.73	10.14	7.88	54	22.81	18.10	13.98
32	13.05	10.40	8.08	55		18.59	14.35
33	13.37	10.66	8.28	56		19.10	14.74
34	13.71	10.92	8.49	57		19.63	15.14
35	14.05	11.20	8.70	58		20.19	15.56
36	14.41	11.48	8.91	59		20.78	15.99
37	14.77	11.76	9.14	60			16.45
38	15.14	12.06	9.36	61			16.94
39	15.53	12.36	9.60	62			17.45
40	15.92	12.67	9.84	63			17.99
41	16.32	12.99	10.08	64			18.57
42	16.73	13.32	10.34				

Table 6.3 Women in private sector schemes

Age last birthday at dismissal	Normal retirement age – women			Age last birthday at dismissal	Normal retirement age – women		
	55	60	65		55	60	65
20 and under	7.37	5.79	4.41	43	13.76	10.79	8.20
21	7.57	5.94	4.53	44	14.15	11.08	8.42
22	7.78	6.11	4.66	45	14.54	11.39	8.66
23	7.99	6.27	4.78	46	14.95	11.71	8.90
24	8.21	6.44	4.91	47	15.37	12.04	9.14
25	8.43	6.62	5.05	48	15.80	12.37	9.40
26	8.67	6.80	5.18	49	16.25	12.72	9.66
27	8.90	6.99	5.33	50	16.71	13.08	9.93
28	9.15	7.18	5.47	51	17.19	13.45	10.21
29	9.40	7.38	5.62	52	17.69	13.84	10.49
30	9.66	7.58	5.77	53	18.20	14.23	10.79
31	9.92	7.79	5.93	54	18.73	14.65	11.10
32	10.20	8.00	6.09	55		15.07	11.42
33	10.48	8.22	6.26	56		15.52	11.75
34	10.77	8.45	6.43	57		15.98	12.10
35	11.06	8.68	6.61	58		16.46	12.45
36	11.37	8.92	6.79	59		16.96	12.83
37	11.68	9.16	6.97	60			13.22
38	12.00	9.41	7.16	61			13.63
39	12.34	9.67	7.36	62			14.05
40	12.68	9.94	7.56	63			14.50
41	13.03	10.21	7.77	64			14.98
42	13.39	10.49	7.98				

Table 6.4 Women in public sector schemes

Age last birthday at dismissal	Normal retirement age – women			Age last birthday at dismissal	Normal retirement age – women		
	55	*60*	*65*		*55*	*60*	*65*
20 and under	9.94	7.97	6.22	43	17.58	14.07	10.97
21	10.19	8.17	6.38	44	18.03	14.42	11.24
22	10.45	8.37	6.54	45	18.49	14.79	11.53
23	10.71	8.58	6.70	46	18.96	15.16	11.82
24	10.97	8.79	6.87	47	19.45	15.55	12.12
25	11.25	9.01	7.04	48	19.95	15.95	12.43
26	11.53	9.24	7.21	49	20.46	16.36	12.74
27	11.82	9.47	7.39	50	20.99	16.78	13.07
28	12.11	9.70	7.58	51	21.54	17.22	13.41
29	12.42	9.94	7.76	52	22.11	17.67	13.75
30	12.73	10.19	7.96	53	22.69	18.13	14.11
31	13.05	10.45	8.16	54	23.29	18.61	14.48
32	13.37	10.71	8.36	55		19.11	14.86
33	13.71	10.98	8.57	56		19.62	15.26
34	14.05	11.25	8.78	57		20.15	15.67
35	14.40	11.53	9.00	58		20.70	16.10
36	14.77	11.82	9.22	59		21.28	16.54
37	15.14	12.12	9.45	60			17.00
38	15.52	12.42	9.69	61			17.48
39	15.91	12.73	9.93	62			17.98
40	16.31	13.05	10.18	63			18.51
41	16.72	13.38	10.44	64			19.07
42	17.15	13.72	10.70				

Appendix 7
Tables of factors to be applied to the standard contribution rate to assess the age specific contribution rate

Table 7.1 Men

Age last birthday at dismissal	Normal retirement age – men			Age last birthday at dismissal	Normal retirement age – men		
	55	*60*	*65*		*55*	*60*	*65*
20 and under	0.77	0.74	0.71	43	1.09	1.04	1.00
21	0.78	0.75	0.72	44	1.11	1.06	1.01
22	0.79	0.76	0.73	45	1.12	1.08	1.03
23	0.80	0.77	0.74	46	1.14	1.09	1.05
24	0.82	0.78	0.75	47	1.16	1.11	1.06
25	0.83	0.79	0.76	48	1.18	1.13	1.08
26	0.84	0.81	0.77	49	1.20	1.15	1.09
27	0.85	0.82	0.78	50	1.22	1.16	1.11
28	0.87	0.83	0.80	51	1.24	1.18	1.13
29	0.88	0.84	0.81	52	1.26	1.20	1.15
30	0.89	0.86	0.82	53	1.28	1.22	1.17
31	0.91	0.87	0.83	54	1.30	1.24	1.18
32	0.92	0.88	0.84	55		1.27	1.20
33	0.93	0.90	0.86	56		1.29	1.22
34	0.95	0.91	0.87	57		1.31	1.24
35	0.96	0.92	0.88	58		1.33	1.27
36	0.98	0.94	0.90	59		1.36	1.29
37	0.99	0.95	0.91	60			1.31
38	1.01	0.97	0.93	61			1.34
39	1.02	0.98	0.94	62			1.37
40	1.04	1.00	0.95	63			1.39
41	1.06	1.01	0.97	64			1.42
42	1.07	1.03	0.98				

Table 7.2 Women

Age last birthday at dismissal	Normal retirement age – women			Age last birthday at dismissal	Normal retirement age – women		
	55	*60*	*65*		*55*	*60*	*65*
20 and under	0.77	0.74	0.70	43	1.09	1.04	0.99
21	0.78	0.75	0.71	44	1.11	1.06	1.00
22	0.79	0.76	0.72	45	1.12	1.08	1.02
23	0.81	0.77	0.73	46	1.14	1.09	1.03
24	0.82	0.78	0.75	47	1.16	1.11	1.05
25	0.83	0.80	0.76	48	1.18	1.13	1.07
26	0.84	0.81	0.77	49	1.20	1.14	1.08
27	0.86	0.82	0.78	50	1.21	1.16	1.10
28	0.87	0.83	0.79	51	1.23	1.18	1.12
29	0.88	0.85	0.80	52	1.25	1.20	1.14
30	0.90	0.86	0.81	53	1.28	1.22	1.15
31	0.91	0.87	0.83	54	1.30	1.24	1.17
32	0.92	0.88	0.84	55		1.26	1.19
33	0.94	0.90	0.85	56		1.28	1.21
34	0.95	0.91	0.86	57		1.30	1.23
35	0.96	0.92	0.88	58		1.33	1.25
36	0.98	0.94	0.89	59		1.35	1.27
37	0.99	0.95	0.90	60			1.30
38	1.01	0.97	0.92	61			1.32
39	1.02	0.98	0.93	62			1.35
40	1.04	1.00	0.95	63			1.37
41	1.06	1.01	0.96	64			1.40
42	1.07	1.03	0.97				